SMART PILLS

E. Martin Pedersen

Smart pills. Take one every day. They'll make you smart. If you don't believe it you don't need them. You're already smart.

bless the hand that holds the pen
mighty and sharp —
it's time for strong words

tell your life story
so even a doll's face
comes alive

great poets bide
poor and unknown
struggling towards the end

the cross of mortality
points in every direction
north south east and west

may the paper strip
in your fortune cookie
always be blank

red or green
the button will be pressed

you have friends
all over the world
that you don't know

it takes a long time to learn a new language
longer still to forget one's own

immigration becomes exile
when you know the bastards
all too well

in every country
including New Guinea —
boring biased talk

you read the morning news
you get depressed ...
don't read the news

natural disasters
separate friends
unite families

if you're not over-weight
or don't speak English
are you okay?

television is on us
as smallpox blankets
to native tribes

can I please think
my own private thoughts
without tele-intervention?

all drugs are mistakes but
it may take generations
to overcome the urge

artists intrigue
by hiding the I am
under layers of color

money has no warmth, no pride
lying dead
in banks made of stone

numbers rise and numbers fall
they mean nothing —
the accounting distraction

order needs disorder
disorder needs order —
a marriage

if I don't meet
my dead-line
will I die?

what I want is not
what I think I want

heaven must be upwards
that's where flames point

the vase and/or the women?
relax
let them see you

raise a glass
take a photo —
that's celebration

a tight wedding dress
leaves marks on the skin

the silent strength captured
in photographs of ancestors
makes us ashamed

rub the puppy's belly
counterclockwise
to unwind two at once

crack a nut to find what's inside —
grab a hammer, a nut
crack it

a dab of ointment
and the ache disappears
with careful rubbing

garden, knit, toss a ball
anything not electric —
going back is going forward

if you seek advice
on important topics
drink tea first

plan a trip
then take a different one
open-heartedly

comb your mustache upwards
to get that certain effect

talking in the mirror
cures the silent treatment
one gives to oneself

hypertension —
a child's prophesy
in the adult fulfilled

when stuck in the theatre of the absurd
recite in a language you don't speak

when no one does the job right
competence becomes the enemy

when upstairs yells
downstairs raises the volume

something funny
in every tense or tragic situation —
the funeral fart

artichokes —
two hours to prepare
ten minutes to eat

we work to excess
to push shopping carts
to eat banquets
to fill toilets and trash bins

exam day —
stay calm
or fake it

a beautiful bag
that weighs too much —
you don't need that

teach a child to tie a bow —
ordinary usefulness

computer failure, lost files —
get to a window
watch outside leaves fall

it's so pleasant
when people you know
say hello to you
in the road

too many shops
one on every corner
as if we couldn't walk

cities without cars —
such a civilized way
to save the earth

walk over deserts oceans
mountains lakes volcanoes
forests filling with snow ...
then rest

with special skins you can ski uphill —
defying gravity
by ingenuity

don't offend the mountain
by complaining of the climb

if we lived on the moon
we would whine about craters

a new cane plus sturdy boots
equals altitude and attitude

make the moon your friend,
never be lonely

find the right spot
lie down naked
let each falling cherry blossom
bless your skin

hunger and thirst
make the berry sweeter
the thorn forgiven

the fish in the net
don't know they're caught
until the fisher pulls

no swan ever had too much water
but bees can get drunk

small deer turn to look
mighty elk stampede away

homo sapiens, the destroyer —
other animals have reasons
for everything they do

a strong family tree …
swing from a branch
or climb for perspective

eliminate waste as plants do —
nourishing life by day
expelling poison by night

study, learn
the languages of animals
incapable of lying

when you want to talk about existence
talk about birds

take recess
come back
ready to learn